WIDE EYED EDITIONS

# CONTENTS

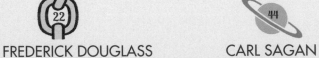

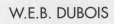

## AUTHOR'S NOTE

The phrase "boys will be boys" has bothered me for a long time. I usually hear the phrase used when boys misbehave. We say **"BOYS WILL BE BOYS"** when boys and men act out, don't listen, or hurt others. We say it as if these behaviors are exactly what we should expect.

But we can expect more. Phrases like "boys will be boys" set us up to think about boys in narrow and limited ways, so it is incredibly important for us to tell the stories of people who have defied those expectations. It is important that we tell the stories of boys and men who do things like care deeply about others, stand up for what is right, and express themselves in creative and exciting ways.

This book tells some of those stories. Through the lives of 30 people, this book aims to show that there are countless ways to be boys and men beyond what we think when we hear "boys will be boys." These stories need to be shared so that everyone growing into manhood or living alongside growing boys and men can recognize that **there is no one way to be a man**.

Instead of a single model of how a boy can grow into a man, this book offers 30 stories of people whose lives demonstrate that there are endless possibilities—that boys and men can do and be so much more than what we think of when we say things like "boys will be boys."

So, turn the page to discover a world of inspirational change-makers, teachers, peacemakers, artists, and more.

It is my hope that as you read this book you find yourself thinking **"BOY OH BOY"** because your idea of what it means to be a boy or man just got a little broader, or "boy oh boy" because you found an example of a boy or a man that you can look up to.


Dr. Cliff Leek
Assistant Professor of Sociology at the University of Northern Colorado

BORN: **JULY 9, 1937**

# David Hockney is a painter, printmaker, and photographer.

David was born in Bradford, England in 1937. He was interested in art from a young age, especially the greats such as Picasso and Matisse. In fact, when he was a kid he was often caught drawing cartoons in Sunday School.

Even as he got older David often doodled and daydreamed in classes – and his grades slipped because of it. But, he knew that art was what he wanted to do. So he started working to be transferred to an art school. His parents encouraged him, and he finally got his wish at age 16.

He made many friends at art school but dedicated most of his attention to his work. After getting his diploma, he was accepted into the Royal College of Art in London – a huge honor! While he was there he worked to develop his own painting style and started getting attention from art critics and buyers. He even won a gold medal from the RCA in 1962.

Inspired by the Hollywood movies of his childhood, he moved to Los Angeles, California, in 1964. He was bewitched by Los Angeles, with its sunny weather, stunning houses, and deep blue swimming pools. So much so, that he created a whole series of swimming pool paintings, including one called *A BIGGER SPLASH*. He used a new kind of paint, acrylic, in these paintings and made them very bright, capturing the California sunshine on the water.

David also used his art to share something important about himself. Through paint, he told the world that he was gay: he loved men. His art told people it was okay to be gay. This was a very brave thing to do in the 1960s, because there was a lot more discrimination against gay men at that time.

David has been honored with a number of awards for his amazing artistry. He is an example of a person who worked very hard to pursue his dreams and become the best artist he could be. He is successful because he stayed true to what and who he loved.

*"What an artist is trying to do for people is bring them closer to something.*

*"Float like a butterfly ..."*

## Muhammad Ali was a boxing champion and civil rights activist.

When Muhammad Ali was born, his name was Cassius Clay. Cassius grew up with his parents and younger brother in Louisville, Kentucky. His father painted signs for a living and his mother was a cleaner. Cassius experienced a lot of discrimination when he was a young boy, because he was African American, at a time when Kentucky was racially segregated. Segregation meant that white and black people were separated.

When Cassius was 12 years old, someone stole his prized possession: his new red-and-white bicycle. He was upset, and went to tell local police officer, Joe Martin. The police officer happened to run a boxing gym, and offered to teach him how to fight. Cassius joined Joe's gym and started to learn how to box. He worked hard, and quickly became a very good boxer, winning his first fight in 1954. Six years later, when he was 18 years old, he became an Olympic gold medalist.

In 1961 Cassius became involved in a religion called The Nation of Islam, and in 1964 he changed his name to **MUHAMMAD ALI** to match his beliefs. Muhammad means "beloved of God" or "worthy of praise" in Arabic.

1964 was also the year that Muhammad became Heavyweight Champion of the World, conquering his opponents with revolutionary techniques, smart strategy and poetic talk.

But even though he was now considered one of the best boxers in the world, Muhammad used his fame to speak out on many important issues he cared about—**fighting with words instead of his body.** One of the issues he spoke out about was racism. Muhammad was proud of his heritage as an African American, and he became a symbol of pride and resistance for many people.

Muhammad also spoke out against the Vietnam War. In 1966, he refused to be drafted into the US military because he believed the war was unjust and against his beliefs. However, in 1967, he was arrested for refusing to fight in the war. He was not allowed to box again for almost four years.

Muhammad was punished for standing up for what he believed in – but he was fearless. It never stopped him from doing what he felt was right.

*"Service to others is the rent you pay for your room here on Earth."*

*"...sting like a bee."*

# nelson mandela

BORN: **JULY 18, 1918** DIED: **DECEMBER 5, 2013**

## Nelson Mandela was the first black president of South Africa.

Nelson grew up in the Thembu royal family in Mvezo, South Africa. As a young boy, Nelson worked herding cattle and spent his free time playing outside with friends. His parents did not know how to read or write but they sent him to school so that he could learn. Nelson discovered a love for learning that lasted through life.

When he was young his father died, and his mother sent him to live with the political leader, Chief Jongintaba Dalindyebo. While there, he spent time listening to and learning from visitors to the palace who taught him a lot about African history.

When Nelson was 19, his interest in African history grew. Over the next few years Nelson learned more about law. He learned about the effect that the British Empire's rule was having on South Africa and how apartheid (the separation of people based on skin color) was affecting black South Africans. Black South Africans were not allowed to vote, did not have access to good schools, and were met with violence.

In the 1940s, Nelson started to help young people challenge apartheid and the British Empire's rule. He helped found an organization, the **AFRICAN NATIONAL CONGRESS YOUTH LEAGUE**, in 1944 to work toward those goals. He looked to Mahatma Gandhi's successful movement to free India as an example of how to work nonviolently for change.

He organized protests and pushed for change but the government started to hurt protestors. Because the government was violently resisting change, Nelson helped create another organization, which used violence to fight against racial inequality. Nelson was arrested for his involvement with this resistance and spent over 26 years in prison. Most of this time was spent in a tiny cell on Robben Island.

When he was released from prison, Nelson continued his work to end apartheid in South Africa, and he was awarded the Nobel Peace Prize. But Nelson's hard work really paid off in 1994, when—for the first time in South Africa's history—people of all races were allowed to vote. That year, he was elected as President. He was the first black president of South Africa and served until he retired in 1999.

When Nelson died in 2013, he had become not only a beloved leader in his country, but a symbol of hope, equality and freedom around the world.

POWER TO THE PEOPLE

ALFR. NOBEL
NAT. MDCCC XXXIII
OB. MDCCC XCVI

*I am, because we all are.*

BORN: **JUNE 7, 1958** DIED: **APRIL 21, 2016**

# Prince was a singer, songwriter and forward-thinking musical innovator.

He was born in Minneapolis, Minnesota to a musical family. His father was a jazz musician and his mother was a singer, who met in the same band they named Prince after: The Prince Rogers Trio.

At school, Prince played many sports—but his real passion was music. He followed in his parents' footsteps and taught himself how to play the piano, drums, and guitar. He became obsessed, and started writing music on his father's piano when he was only seven years old.

His parents divorced when he was ten, so Prince split his time between his mother's house and his father's house, before eventually running away to live with neighbors. His neighbor's son, Andre Anderson, became a bandmate in his first group: *GRAND CENTRAL*.

In 1978, record bosses recognized his musical talent, and 20-year-old Prince created his first solo album. He played all the instruments on the record and became a huge success.

Over the rest of his life, Prince released over 40 albums and sold over 100 million records. He mixed rock, pop and funk music to create a new sound and connected with fans across the globe.

But Prince was not only famous for his music: he had his own style of dressing and acting that challenged stereotypes about the way men should look and behave. He was not afraid to do things that other people thought were feminine, and he showed other men that it was okay for them to do them too.

Prince used his fame to speak about racial inequality. In 2015, he wrote a song and held a concert in tribute to Freddie Gray, an African-American man who died in police custody. The lyrics of the song say "enough is enough, it's time for love."

Millions of people mourned when Prince died in 2016, because he was such a great musician and inspiration. Prince had become an idol for many by following his passions and staying true to himself, throughout his life.

*"Albums still matter. Like books and black lives, albums still matter."*

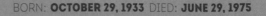

## Richard Loving protested the unjust law against interracial marriage.

Richard was born in Central Point, Virginia, a small rural town. When Richard was 17 years old he met Mildred Jeter. They quickly became friends and after a while, they started to fall in love. Soon after, they were ready to get married.

But for the two of them, one white and one African and Native American, getting married was not a simple thing to do. In Virginia, where they lived, there was a law that made it illegal for people of different races to get married. Richard and Mildred knew that the law was wrong and unfair, but they decided to get married anyway. They journeyed to Washington, D.C., where interracial marriage was legal. They got married on June 2, 1958 and then traveled back to Virginia.

A few weeks later the local sheriff stormed into their house in the middle of the night. Under the glare of his flashlight, he arrested the couple for breaking the law against interracial marriage. A judge ruled that if they wanted to stay married they had to leave, and stay out of, Virginia. So, they left their home and moved to Washington, D.C.

In 1964, Richard and Mildred started working with the American Civil Liberties Union (ACLU), a group of lawyers that fights for civil rights, to start a lawsuit, called **LOVING V. VIRGINIA**, which made it all the way to the United States Supreme Court!

In 1967, the Supreme Court agreed with Richard and Mildred that the law was not fair. They decided that throughout the US the government could not stop people from getting married because of the color of their skin. Virginia's law was struck down and Richard and Mildred could finally live openly in Virginia as husband and wife.

Together Richard and Mildred raised three children named Sidney, Donald, and Peggy. Those children got to grow up in a world that was more fair because Richard and Mildred had fought to change an unjust law.

Richard died in 1975 but today the name "Loving" is a reminder that the law should not stand in the way of love.

*"Tell the court I love my wife, and it is just unfair that I can't live with her in Virginia."*

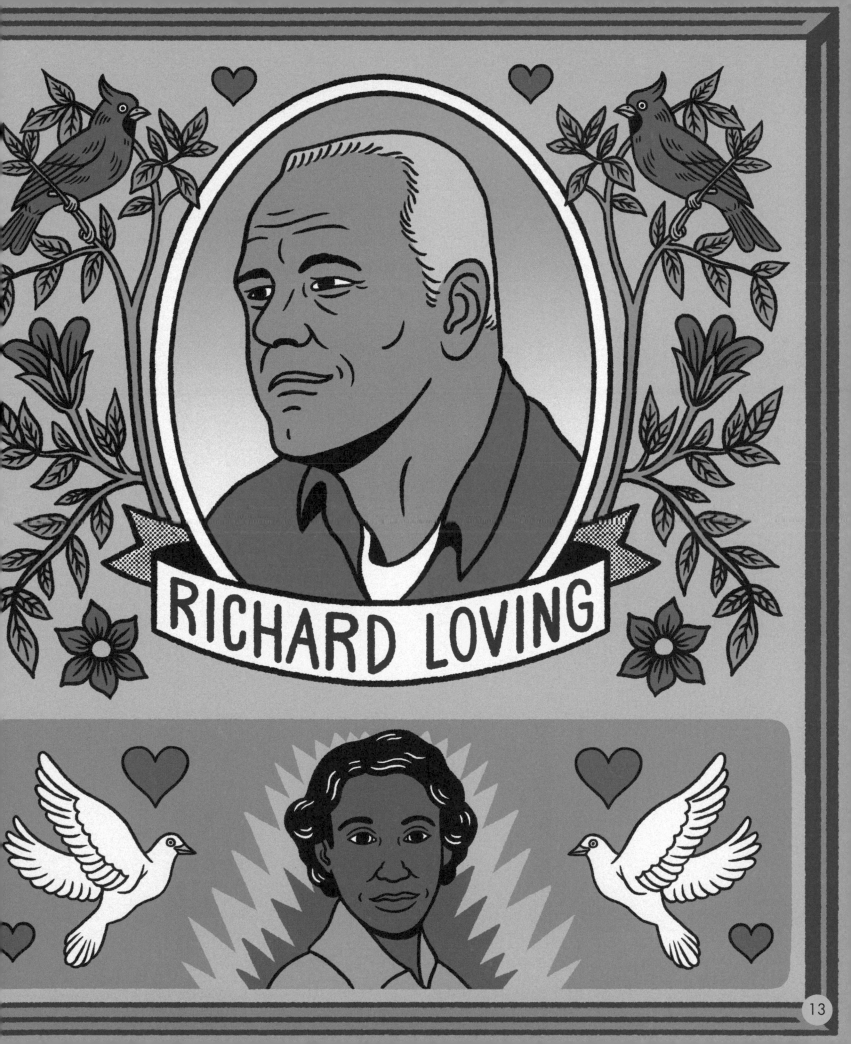

RICHARD LOVING

BORN: **MARCH 31, 1927**
DIED: **APRIL 23, 1993**

**César Chávez was a leader in the struggle for the rights of workers and immigrants, as well as for civil rights more broadly.**

César was born into a Mexican-American family and he spent his early years living in Yuma, Arizona. His parents owned a ranch and a small grocery store there and they worked very hard.

But in the 1930s, his family lost almost everything they owned, including their home. This was the time of the Great Depression, a period in history when many people around the world lost their jobs and homes because of an economic crisis. After losing their home, his family moved to California and became farm workers. They harvested crops year-round and would move from place to place depending on what needed to be picked. This was a big change for César and his family because they no longer had one place to call home.

Farm work was very hard and often unsafe and César cared a lot about the other workers. When he was a teenager he often drove other workers to and from the doctor when they needed help. His passion for caring about those around him came to define his life.

In 1952, when César was 25, he became a community organizer. He helped Mexican Americans register to vote, so they could have a say in the laws that affected their lives. He started rallying people to improve the conditions for farm workers. Through his work organizing farm workers, he met and became friends with Dolores Huerta, another iconic community organizer and civil rights activist. They worked brilliantly together and became a dynamic duo. In 1962, they founded the National Farm Workers Association, an organization that worked to make sure that farmworkers were paid fairly and had safer working conditions. They forced employers to provide things like housing and healthcare.

After César passed away in 1993, he was awarded with the Presidential Medal of Freedom, the highest award the United States government gives to civilians. César Chávez is an example of how a person who cares deeply about others can become a leader and accomplish great things.

*"You are never strong enough that you don't need help."*

CÉSAR CHÁVEZ

THURGOOD MARSHALL

BORN: **JULY 2, 1908** DIED: **JANUARY 24, 1993**

# Thurgood Marshall was the first African-American justice on the Supreme Court.

Thurgood was born in Baltimore, Maryland, where he grew up with his older brother and parents. When Thurgood was young, his father would bring him and his brother to the local court house to watch cases. They would hotly debate the outcomes, sometimes arguing five out of seven nights a week. Thurgood learned how to choose his words carefully and to defend his opinions with conviction. He also started to learn about the law.

Growing up, Thurgood experienced racial discrimination because he was African American. Baltimore was segregated, which meant there were different rules for black and white Americans. Racial segregation was legal, and these early experiences would later make him passionate about civil rights.

Thurgood went on to study at Lincoln University. He became a member of the debate team, further developing the skill to form his own opinions and defend them.

After finishing college, Thurgood decided he wanted to become a lawyer. But the University of Maryland Law School refused to let African Americans attend. So, he went to Howard University School of Law, which specifically served African-American students. He graduated at the top of his class and became a fully-fledged lawyer in 1933.

In Thurgood's first court case he sued the University of Maryland for not letting black students attend. **And he won!** Thurgood quickly became one of the most important leaders in the fight for civil rights. He was the leading lawyer for the National Association for the Advancement of Colored People (NAACP), one of the most significant organizations working for civil rights in the US.

Thurgood also worked on a landmark case, ***BROWN V. BOARD OF EDUCATION***. He told the Supreme Court that it should not be legal for schools to be segregated. And he won again! Then, in 1967, he became the first African American to serve on the Supreme Court. For 24 long years, he worked to advance justice for people of color in the US.

Thurgood changed the world for the better, using his experience of discrimination as fuel and his education as power. He got to the heart of the justice system and struck down legalized racism wherever he could.

"WHERE YOU SEE WRONG OR INEQUALITY OR INJUSTICE, SPEAK OUT, BECAUSE THIS IS YOUR COUNTRY! THIS IS YOUR DEMOCRACY. MAKE IT. PROTECT IT. PASS IT ON."

# John Muir was a wilderness campaigner.

BORN: **APRIL 21, 1838**
DIED: **DECEMBER 24, 1914**

John was born in a small town called Dunbar on the coast of Scotland. He grew up there with his seven siblings and parents, who were farmers. When he was a young boy he spent his free time taking walks with his grandfather, exploring the countryside, and hunting for birds' nests. He would compete with his friends to see who could find the most nests. It was in these early days that John first fell in love with nature.

When John was 11 years old, he moved to the US with his family and started a new farm in Wisconsin. He spent his teenage years there before enrolling at the University of Wisconsin. At university, John was introduced to botany (the study of plants) which deepened his understanding of the natural world.

In 1864, John moved to Southern Ontario, in Canada, to be near his brother Daniel. John spent the warm parts of the year exploring nature. He hiked in forests and swamps, collecting and taking notes on all the flora and fauna he found.

He moved back to the US in 1866 and took up work in a wagon wheel factory in Indianapolis.

His eyesight was damaged in an accident at the factory and he had to spend several weeks in the dark while his eyes healed. Spending that much time in the dark made him appreciate everything he could see in nature even more. From that point on, he decided he would be a fearless explorer and protector of the natural world.

After exploring the world he came to call California his home. He settled in San Francisco in 1868 and spent the rest of his life trekking through the mountains and deserts of California, then writing books and articles about his adventures. He encountered boiling springs, huge deep pools, and cool mountains. He wrote about the beauty of nature, but he also wrote about the damage that people were doing to the environment.

John dreamt of a world where wild spaces would be protected. So, he led efforts to create the first national parks in the US, including **YOSEMITE**, the Grand Canyon and Sequoia National Park.

John died in 1914 but he is remembered as a leader. He became known as "John of the Mountains" and **"Father of the National Parks"** because of his tireless work as a wilderness protector.

JOHN MUIR

5¢

"The mountains are calling and I must go."

LEBRON JAMES

BORN: **DECEMBER 30, 1984**

# LeBron James might be the best player that basketball has ever seen.

He was born in 1984 in Akron, Ohio where he grew up with his mother, Gloria Marie James. Gloria had a hard time getting and keeping jobs when LeBron was younger, so she sent LeBron to live with Frank Walker, a local American football coach, and his family. Frank got LeBron involved in sports when he was nine years old.

LeBron quickly became a basketball star. Playing together with a team of his close friends, they won the Amateur Athletic Union National Championship Tournament in 1999. His team then won the state championship game three out of the four years that he was in high school.

In 2003 he joined the National Basketball Association (NBA) as a member of the Cleveland Cavaliers and was named Rookie of the Year in his first year. Since he joined the NBA, LeBron has become one of the best basketball players in history. He has led his teams to win three NBA championships, has been named the NBA's Most Valuable Player (MVP) four times, and played on three Olympic gold-medal winning basketball teams. His advice to young players is: **"You have to be able to accept failure to get better."**

While LeBron's basketball achievements have been extraordinary, he has also done amazing things off the court. He has consistently used both his influence as a role model and his money to support positive change in the world. In 2005 he created the ***LEBRON JAMES FAMILY FOUNDATION*** which raises money for a wide range of causes. He donated over two million dollars to help build the National Museum of African American History and Culture and donated a lot of money to create scholarships and support for students. In recent years he also has started to speak out about issues of racial inequality.

In 2017 he received two important awards for his work outside of basketball. First, the NBA awarded him the J. Walter Kennedy Citizenship Award for the season. This award is given to the NBA player who has used their fame and fortune to give back to the community. Second, the NAACP gave him the Jackie Robinson Award, an award that the NAACP rarely gives out, which honored LeBron for his work on social justice and civil rights issues.

LeBron is a great example of how powerful people can speak out for, and support, those who don't have the same resources. LeBron is known today not only for being one of the best basketball players of all time, but also for being an advocate for others.

FREDERICK DOUGLASS

BORN: **c. FEBRUARY, 1818** DIED: **FEBRUARY 20, 1895**

## Frederick Douglass was a civil rights activist.

Frederick was born in Maryland, US, at a time when slavery was still allowed and common. When he was a child, Frederick was enslaved along with his parents. At a very young age his owner separated him from his family and moved him to a plantation in Baltimore.

At the time it was not common to teach enslaved people how to read, because owners thought that they would become too smart and try to be free. However, when Frederick was about 12 years old, one of his owners, Sophia Auld, taught him the alphabet and the beginnings of how to read. Once Frederick had learned the basics, he started to teach himself by paying close attention whenever he was around other people who were reading or writing. Eventually he started to teach other slaves how to read and write too.

After learning to read, Frederick frequently attempted to escape slavery. At first he was unsuccessful, but in 1838, when Frederick was 18 years old, he met and fell in love with a free African-American woman named Anna Murray, who helped him escape. He got on a train out of Baltimore and disguised himself as a sailor, with an outfit Anna had given him, to make the journey to Pennsylvania, where slavery was not allowed. From Pennsylvania,

he continued traveling all the way to New York City. When he got to New York City, Frederick and Anna got married.

They then moved to Massachusetts, where Frederick became a preacher in 1839. As a preacher, Frederick was able to practice his public speaking skills and share his beliefs. He joined the abolitionist movement to end slavery, and started to travel and give public speeches about the importance of ending slavery and supporting African Americans' right to vote. Many people at the time did not agree with Frederick on these issues and in 1843, he was attacked by people who supported slavery. That did not stop him from speaking out.

Frederick also believed that women's rights were very important. In 1848, he was one of 40 men, and the only African American, to attend the Seneca Falls Convention, the first large meeting of people to organize for women's rights. He made an important speech at that convention urging everyone there to sign a statement supporting women's right to vote.

Throughout his life, Frederick used his powerful voice to support equality and rights for all people. Even though Frederick died in 1895, he is remembered today as one of the most influential voices for equality in US history. The book he wrote about his life, ***NARRATIVE OF THE LIFE OF FREDERICK DOUGLASS***, is one of the most important books in American history.

**"IT IS EASIER TO BUILD STRONG CHILDREN THAN TO REPAIR BROKEN MEN."**

PAT MANUEL

## Patricio Manuel is the first transgender professional boxer in the US.

Patricio grew up outside of Los Angeles, California. He was raised by his mother and grandmother, who both worked very hard. His mother was a waitress and his grandmother had two jobs, including working at a hospital.

When Patricio was young, people treated him as if he was a girl. His name was Patricia, but he never felt like a girl. As he got older and his body changed, it became even clearer to him that the identity of being a girl that he had been given did not fit how he thought of himself.

When Patricio was 16 years old, he asked his grandmother for boxing lessons for Christmas. He wanted to start boxing because he thought boxing would give him a way to feel more connected to his body. He also wanted to emulate the style and masculinity of the characters he saw on TV and in video games.

He got his wish. Patricio loved boxing and worked very hard at it. But, it wasn't easy. He lost his first match in about 30 seconds. But that loss just motivated Patricio to work even harder.

When Patricio started boxing competitively people saw him as a woman, so he competed in the women's boxing competitions. He became a five-time national amateur champion, represented the US in international competitions, and competed in the first ever women's Olympic boxing trials. On his way home from the trials, he thought a lot about his identity and how people saw him. He decided **it was time for other people to see him the way he saw himself—as a man.**

Over the next two years Patricio transitioned from his life being seen as a woman to being seen as a man. That transition included taking hormones, having surgery, and changing his name from Patricia to Patricio.

Just like when he started boxing, the beginning wasn't easy. When he came out as a man, the gym where he trained no longer welcomed him. But, of course, he did not let any of that stop him. Patricio started working with a new coach, who supported him and embraced him for who he was.

Patricio won his first fight as a man and also became the first person in professional boxing to transition from fighting in the women's division to fighting in the men's. Patricio is still training and fighting today.

"IT HAS ABSOLUTELY BEEN WORTH THIS JOURNEY TO LIVE PUBLICLY AS MY TRUE SELF."

BORN: **JANUARY 5, 1941**

## Hayao Miyazaki is an animator, screenwriter, and film director.

Hayao was born in Tokyo, Japan. His father was the director of a company that made fighter planes during World War Two. Young Hayao was surrounded by airplanes and design drawings and learned to love the way they looked. At night, he dreamt of flying above the cities of Japan among the clouds.

Growing up during World War Two, Hayao's family had to move around because of bombings. Then, when Hayao was about six years old, his mother got sick with a disease called spinal tuberculosis. She had to stay in the hospital for several years to receive care.

The war and his mother's illness were hard for Hayao and he found comfort in art. He started drawing pictures of airplanes and other flying ships at a young age. Inspired by the machines that he had seen during the war, Hayao drew tanks and battleships too. He dreamed of becoming an artist for a style of Japanese comic books called **MANGA**.

Hayao knew that he was good at drawing objects... but he was not so good at drawing people—so he practiced. He practiced a lot. He would spend his free time going to visit his art teacher to practice drawing in his studio.

In 1963, when Hayao was 22 years old, he got a job working as an artist for the first of many movies that he would work on, *Doggie March*. Hayao started to write his own movies in addition to animating other people's movies and animating manga comics.

While developing his animation skills, he fell in love with another artist, Akemi Ōta. Together they had two sons, Gorō and Keisuke. Both of his sons grew up to be artists and have been involved in making TV shows and movies, too.

In 1985, Hayao and three friends started their own film studio, Studio Ghibli. With magical stories and beautiful art, they made some of Japan's most famous movies, including **SPIRITED AWAY.**

Seeing the bombings during the war had a big impact on Hayao, and as a result, many of his movies have anti-war themes. They are also well known for having important female characters.

Hayao will leave an important legacy in his work. He writes scripts that have girls as heroes, which has not always been common. He said that "Many of my movies have strong female leads— brave, self-sufficient girls that don't think twice about fighting for what they believe in with all their heart. They'll need a friend, or a supporter, but never a savior. **Any woman is just as capable of being a hero as any man."**

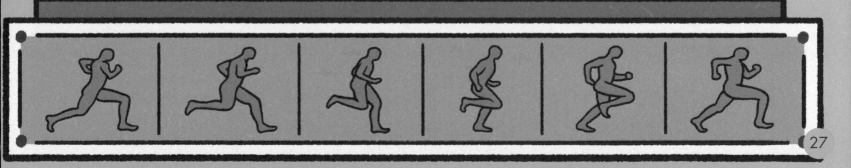

Oscar Wilde

BORN: **OCTOBER 16, 1854**
DIED: **NOVEMBER 30, 1900**

# Oscar Wilde was a famous poet and playwright.

When Oscar was young, his mother used to read him poems. Born in Dublin, Ireland, he was inspired by the words of Irish authors and activists and began to write poetry on his own.

Oscar wrote poetry all through school. He was a great student, and when he was 17 years old, he won a royal scholarship to study at Trinity College in Dublin. He had a brilliant mind, and his teachers encouraged him to apply for a scholarship to study at university. He was awarded the scholarship and moved to England to attend Oxford University—one of the best in the country—in 1874.

While he was at Oxford, Oscar won an award for a poem he wrote, called *Ravenna*, and started to write professionally. After he graduated, he moved to London and published his first collection of poetry in 1881.

Over the next two decades, Oscar wrote a lot. Some of the most famous things he wrote were a collection of stories for children: **THE HAPPY PRINCE AND OTHER TALES,** and a novel called *The Picture of Dorian Gray*. At the time, critics were outraged by his novel, but now it is considered a classic. While he was writing, Oscar started to have a relationship with another man, Lord Alfred Douglass. At that time in Britain, it was illegal for two men to be in a relationship.

The father of Lord Alfred Douglass did not like that his son was in a relationship with another man. He publicly accused Oscar of being gay. Oscar was then arrested, put on trial, and sent to prison. Oscar was forced to do hard labor and was not treated well. He became very sick and collapsed, staying in the infirmary for months while he healed.

But Oscar continued writing even while he was in jail. When he was finally released in 1897, he published what he had written. But his time in prison had taken a toll. He never recovered and eventually, in 1900, he passed away.

Today, Oscar is remembered as one of Ireland's greatest writers. He was a man with brilliant wit and talent who was unfairly punished because of who he loved.

In 2017, the British government apologized for the unfair laws that he was punished for breaking, and pardoned him. Today, gay rights have progressed in Britain and around the world.

*"We are all in the gutter but some of us are looking at the stars."*

"MY JOB IS TO LOOK OUT ON THAT WORLD THAT I WRITE ABOUT AND BE AS HONEST AS I POSSIBLY CAN ABOUT THAT WORLD."

BORN: **SEPTEMBER 30, 1975**

# Ta-Nehisi Coates is an award-winning author, comic book writer, and journalist.

When Ta-Nehisi was a child, he read many of the books on his father's bookshelf. He grew up in Baltimore, Maryland with six siblings. His mother was a teacher and his father ran Black Classic Press, a book publisher that gave a platform to work by people of African descent. His parents taught him how important books and writing were when he was very young. When he got in trouble, his mother would make him write essays.

Ta-Nehisi read a lot of comic books when he was a child. He particularly liked Spider-Man and the X-Men because the heroes were seen by other people to be "weirdos and freaks," which is how he sometimes felt about himself. Reading comic books was a way for Ta-Nehisi to escape into a fantasy world.

Baltimore was not an easy place for a kid to grow up in the 1980s. Every day, Ta-Nehisi worried about crime and violence in his community. But during this time, he learned from his parents that it is important to understand how the world works and do what you can to support your community.

Ta-Nehisi's father was an activist who led the Baltimore branch of the Black Panther Party, an organization dedicated to protecting and serving African-American communities. This meant working with the Black Panthers to create free clothing and food programs to support people in need.

After high school, Ta-Nehisi went to Howard University to study, but he left before graduating because he secured the opportunity to work as a journalist.

Ta-Nehisi first started out by working as a reporter for *The Washington City* paper, but many different papers and magazines wanted to publish his voice. His career really started to take off when he started writing for **THE ATLANTIC** in 2008. He wrote about music, sports and culture. Perhaps most importantly, he wrote about what it was like growing up as a young African-American man in the middle of poverty, violence, and racial inequality.

In addition to writing articles for *The Atlantic*, Ta-Nehisi has written three books. His second book, *Between the World and Me*, won the National Book Award for Nonfiction in 2015.

In 2016 he got to fulfill his lifelong dream by becoming a writer of comic books. From 2016 to 2018 he was the writer for the **BLACK PANTHER** comic books, and in 2018 he started writing Captain America comic books, too.

Today, Ta-Nehisi is one of the most important journalists and writers in America. Realistic and honest, his writing educates and challenges people to think in new ways about racial inequality.

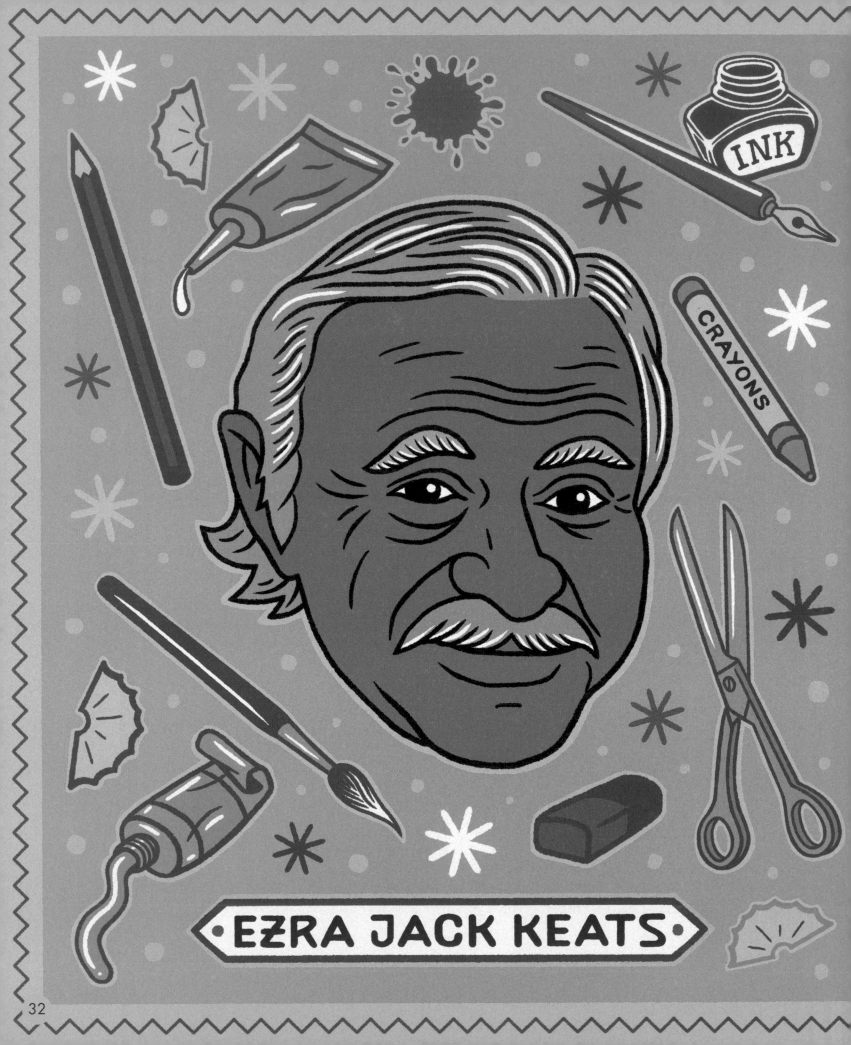

EZRA JACK KEATS

**Ezra Jack Keats wrote one of the most important books of the 20th century—a book for children about a young boy playing in the snow.**

He was born in Brooklyn, New York, where he grew up with his parents and two siblings. His family and friends all called him Jack.

Jack was very artistic as a child and would make pictures out of whatever he could get his hands on. But his father was worried art wouldn't pay the bills, and discouraged Jack from becoming an artist. Jack didn't let that stop him.

All through school Jack made art whenever and however he could. He learned about it at his local library and started to receive recognition for his artistic skill—winning a national art contest and a medal from his school.

Jack planned to study art after finishing high school but, just before his graduation, his father died of a heart attack. Jack found the loss very hard, but he discovered something in his father's wallet that proved that he had supported his art all along—a newspaper clipping of Jack winning an award.

After his father's death, Jack could no longer afford to attend art school—but he knew he had to continue making art. So, he worked as a mural painter and a comic book illustrator, even designing camouflage for the US Army Air Force during World War Two. After the war, Jack was given the opportunity to start illustrating children's books, bringing the words of other authors to life with pictures. He was so good at it, that he created artwork for over 70 books!

Then, in 1960, he started to write his own children's books, and in 1962 **THE SNOWY DAY** was born. It became one of the most famous books ever written. It was important because it was one of the first children's books to have an African-American boy as the hero, and was created with beautiful collage artwork.

According to Jack, he had an African-American boy as the hero **"simply because he should have been there all along."**

Ezra Jack Keats was determined to pursue work he was passionate about—even though it was never easy. And, because of that determination, he created one of the most beautiful children's books ever written.

# Freddie Mercury was a singer-songwriter and frontman of the rock band, Queen.

Farrokh Bulsara spent most of his childhood living in India. His parents wanted him to learn to play music and he started taking piano lessons when he was seven years old. He fell in love with music and it became a lifelong passion for him. In fact, he loved music so much that when he was 12 years old he started a band at his school.

The school he went to was a boarding school for boys near Mumbai, India. While he was there he listened to a lot of Western pop music and liked to play rock and roll.

His friends in boarding school started calling him Freddie because many of them had a hard time saying and spelling Farrokh. He ended up liking the name and his family started calling him Freddie too. When he was 17 years old, Freddie and his family moved to England and Freddie started studying art in London. But, while he was in college he was almost always in a band.

After he graduated, he took a lot of different jobs including selling clothes, and working at Heathrow Airport. But in his free time he was always playing music. Between 1964 and 1970 Freddie played in a lot of different bands—but none of them were very successful.

He didn't let that stop him.

In 1970 Freddie started a new band and called it **QUEEN.** He also started using the last name Mercury as a stage name—so he became **Freddie Mercury.**

Queen was a huge hit. The band released their first album in 1973 and their second in 1974.

Their music became incredibly popular. By the 1980s they were playing concerts in completely full stadiums Freddie released 15 albums with Queen and they became one of the best-selling bands of all time. Many of their songs, like "*WE WILL ROCK YOU*" and "*WE ARE THE CHAMPIONS*" are still iconic songs today. Queen, as a group, was inducted into the Rock & Roll Hall of Fame in 2001, and Freddie was inducted into the Songwriters Hall of Fame in 2003.

Freddie was known for being flamboyant and energetic on stage and off. Many today still look to Freddie as the perfect example of what rock and roll should look and sound like.

Freddie is also remembered as a gay icon. He once said in an interview "**I'm as gay as a daffodil!**" He was not afraid to be himself even at a time when there was a lot of discrimination against men who loved other men.

Freddie struggled with a very difficult disease for the later years of his life. In 1986 Freddie was diagnosed with a virus, known as HIV. HIV harms your immune system and stops your body from being able to fight infections and diseases. At that time, there weren't effective treatments for it. Over the next several years Freddie's health got worse. He continued to make music and tried not to show his fans that he was sick.

Freddie passed away in 1991, but before he died he finally told the world about his illness and encouraged people all over the world to work together to find a cure for HIV. His life inspired people to raise money and awareness of the virus at a time when it was desperately needed.

## "I won't be a rock star. I will be a legend."

GRANDMASTER FLASH

# Grandmaster Flash is a pioneering hip hop artist and DJ.

Joseph Saddler was born in Barbados but he grew up in the Bronx in New York City. When Joseph was young his father had a large record collection, featuring a lot of music from the Caribbean, and by African-American musicians. Joseph was intrigued by the collection and used to get in trouble for looking through the records when he wasn't supposed to.

Childhood was hard for Joseph. At a young age he was sent to live in a foster home because his mother was in hospital and his father didn't look after him as he should have done. Joseph did not like living in foster homes and several times he ran away to try to get back to the Bronx. Eventually, he was moved to a foster home 80 miles from the Bronx, making it much harder for him to get back.

At this new foster home, Joseph no longer had access to the exciting music atmosphere that he loved in the Bronx—**so he had to make his own music however he could**. He started working as a DJ for high school dances and did that until his mom was released from the hospital and he was able to move back in with her.

Once he was back in the Bronx, Joseph was still too young to go to many of the disco clubs where the music he loved was being played—but he was able to go to block parties in the South Bronx. He studied the work of earlier DJs, and invented new ways of mixing music on a turntable. By putting his fingers on the vinyl record he changed the music in new and exciting ways.

By day he was going to school and learning about electronics, but by night Joseph started to become known in the Bronx for the amazing things he could do with a turntable. He was given the nickname "Flash" because of how fast his hands moved.

Influenced by the music of the time, he looped beats to give people more time to groove to the dance breaks in the song. He mastered techniques such as backspin, cutting, and phasing—perfecting and building on the work of early DJ pioneers.

Flash started working with rappers to add lyrics to his music. He formed a new group, ***GRANDMASTER FLASH AND THE FURIOUS FIVE***. Together they were some of the founding artists of hip hop.

Grandmaster Flash and the Furious Five started playing regularly and released their first album, ***THE MESSAGE***, in 1982. The Message had important lyrics about the poverty and violence that African Americans experience in America, and became an example of how music, and hip hop in particular, can carry important political messages.

Through his innovation and commentaries on important issues in music, Grandmaster Flash became one of the founders of hip hop and one of the most important musicians of all time. His iconic beats are sampled in many songs today.

"CONQUER YOUR NEIGHBOURHOOD, CONQUER YOUR CITY, CONQUER YOUR COUNTRY, AND THEN GO AFTER THE REST OF THE WORLD."

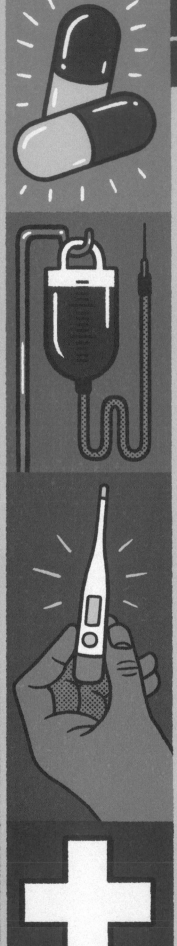

BORN: **FEBRUARY 26, 1915** DIED: **JUNE 7, 2011**

# Luther Christman was the first man to be inducted into the American Nurses Hall of Fame.

Luther was born in Summit Hill, a small town in Pennsylvania. At school, he was always the smallest boy in his class. He often felt like he had to act tough and aggressive to keep up with the other boys. After high school, a local minister recommended that he pursue an education in nursing. At that time the US was in the middle of the Great Depression, so jobs were very hard to find. Nursing school would give Luther a place to live and the ability to work while he studied.

Upon entering the nursing profession, Luther realized that he was doing something that a lot of people thought was inappropriate for a man to do. **Most nurses at that time, and still today, were women.** Many people thought that nursing was work that only women should do. They thought that there must be something wrong with men who wanted to be nurses. In fact, most nursing programs didn't even accept men back then.

Because of the stereotypes about men in nursing, Luther faced a lot of discrimination. For example, Luther was not allowed to study childbirth at the hospital because he was a man. He had to learn as much as he could from textbooks rather than from patients.

When the US entered World War Two, Luther offered to join the Army Nurse Corps to help wounded soldiers but the US Army turned him away. At that time only women were allowed to serve in the Army Nurse Corps. Luther sent letters to every senator in the US asking them to change the rules.

After the war, Luther went back to school. He took as many courses relevant to nursing as he could, but couldn't get a university degree in nursing. They still wouldn't accept men. So he did any nursing work he could and slowly became a leader in the field.

In 1967, Luther became the dean of the nursing school at the University of Michigan —the first man to be dean of a nursing school. Luther spent the rest of his life working to change the way that the world thought about male nurses. In 1974 he helped to start the **NATIONAL MALE NURSE ASSOCIATION**.

He wasn't only concerned about men in nursing though. Luther thought that it was important to encourage all people, regardless of gender or race, to be involved in nursing. He argued that the more diverse nursing was, the more successful nurses would be.

Before Luther died in 2011, the nursing field made it very clear how important his work was. He was inducted into the American Nurses Hall of Fame in 2004, and the American Nurses Association created an award in his name in 2007.

Today Luther is remembered as a pioneer in nursing and as a man who challenged stereotypes about what men can be and what they can do.

# LUTHER CHRISTMAN

MAHATMA GANDHI

## Mohandas Gandhi was the activist who led India to freedom from the British Empire.

Mohandas was born on the coast of India. When he was a child, he liked to read about great leaders, both historical and mythical. He learned lessons from those stories about how good leaders behave and how important it is to stay true to your values. His mother instilled some important Hindu values in Mohandas, including a commitment to non-violence and a belief that all things are connected.

Aged 19 years old, Mohandas traveled to London to study law. His mother was worried that living in London would cause Mohandas to abandon the traditions he grew up with— such as being vegetarian. Mohandas swore that he would not eat any meat, and kept that promise for the three years he was away.

When Mohandas finished studying law, he moved to South Africa to work as a lawyer. He did not plan to stay for long, but then he saw how Indian people were discriminated against. For example, he was not allowed to sit in the same train car as white people. He decided to stay in South Africa and work to end discrimination against Indian people.

Mohandas became an activist. In South Africa, there was a law that required all Indian people to have their fingerprints taken. He encouraged Indian people to defy the unfair law, but he was arrested and sent to jail. When he got out, he continued to work to help Indian people get the right to vote in South Africa.

Mohandas gained a reputation as an activist and community organizer. In 1915, one of his friends from India asked him to come home and work for rights and freedom in India, so he did. At that time the British Empire ruled India and Indian people could not vote for their own government.

Mohandas became a leader in the movement to free India from the British Empire. He organized non-violent activism to resist British rule. He became a hero because his activism was so effective at winning rights. Mohandas' work is one of the main reasons why India was able to win independence from the British Empire in 1947.

Mohandas was given nicknames like **Mahatma**, which means saint, and **Bapu**, an endearing word for father, because he was considered by many people to be the father of India. But, some people were not happy with what Mohandas did. At least five times people who did not like Mohandas' political and religious beliefs tried to kill him. In 1948, one of them succeeded.

Mahatma Gandhi is remembered as a hero who fought for freedom and human rights; who opposed violence of all kinds, and who refused to use violence to achieve his goals.

*"First they ignore you, then they laugh at you, then they fight you, then you win."*

## Bruce Lee was an actor, film director, martial artist, and philosopher.

Lee Jun-Fan, now known as Bruce Lee, was born in San Francisco. When he was only a few months old his family moved to Hong Kong. Bruce grew up there with his four siblings in a wealthy home. Bruce's acting career started when he was a young child. In fact, he was in his first film when he was only three months old!

Even though Bruce's family had a lot of money, their neighborhood was not an easy place to grow up in. At that time, there was a lot of violence, and Bruce got in several fights. His parents decided that he needed to be trained in martial arts.

In 1953, he started learning Kung Fu and one of his first teachers was a master of a style of fighting called Wing Chun. He also joined his school boxing team and won the Hong Kong schools boxing tournament. But he continued to get into street fights—the police were even called once. In 1959, his parents decided that it would be better to get Bruce away from the fighting in Hong Kong, and so they sent him to live in the US.

When he arrived in the US, he went to high school in Seattle and university in Washington. While there, he studied drama and philosophy and met Linda Emery, who he would later marry. Bruce also taught martial arts and opened his own studio.

In 1964, Bruce went to the Long Beach International Karate Championships where he performed some of his signature moves such as "two-finger push-ups" and the "one inch punch" and got the attention of people in Hollywood. In 1966, he was offered the role of Kato, the sidekick in a television series called **THE GREEN HORNET**. That role made him famous. As Kato he got to guest star in several other television shows and movies.

Bruce invented his own martial art, called Jeet Kune Do. He also wrote philosophies that went alongside it, including phrases like: "Empty your mind, be formless, shapeless like water."

While he was living in the US, all of the acting roles that Bruce was given were supporting roles. He was never given the role of the star. So, he decided to move back to Hong Kong. There, he was immediately given leading roles in movies like *The Big Boss*. These movies set box-office records and were incredibly popular in the US, too.

But Bruce passed away suddenly in 1973, when he was only 32 years old. He died just one month before his most successful movie, **ENTER THE DRAGON**, was released. Enter the Dragon is considered by many to be one of the best martial arts movies of all time.

Today Bruce is remembered for being an incredible martial artist and an iconic actor, but also for being a great teacher and a philosopher. Martial arts were not just something that Bruce did as a job. To Bruce, martial arts were a way for him to express himself and think deeply about his role in the world.

"ALWAYS BE YOURSELF, EXPRESS YOURSELF, HAVE FAITH IN YOURSELF."

· CARL SAGAN ·

# Carl Sagan was an astronomer, author, and scientist.

Carl grew up in Brooklyn New York. He was a very curious child. He asked a lot of questions and wanted to know how everything in the world worked. His parents nurtured his curiosity and did their best to help him learn as much as he could.

In 1939, when Carl was four years old, his parents took him to the New York World's Fair, a huge festival celebrating new developments in science, technology, and culture. All of the scientific wonders that Carl saw there were part of what inspired him to become a scientist.

After the fair, Carl asked more and more questions and worked hard to find out the answers to everything he was curious about. **One thing he wondered about was the stars.** He wanted to know what they were and how they worked. So, when he was five years old, his mother gave him a library card. He used his library card to check out books and read about space.

Carl continued to be inquisitive for the rest of his life. In high school his interest in everything helped him to work hard in his classes. He did so well that he was admitted to the University of Chicago when he was only 16 years old.

He worked hard through his time at the University of Chicago, too. He studied physics and earned a Ph.D. by 1960.

Throughout all of his time in school, Carl never forgot how interested he was in the stars and space. He worked with the United States' space agency, **NASA**, and the United States Air Force on top secret projects and wrote important articles about other planets. A lot of what we know about other planets, and especially Venus, is thanks to Carl's research.

While Carl is certainly celebrated for his scientific discoveries, he is even more famous for getting other people excited about science. Carl always wanted everyone else to be just as curious about the world as he was and did everything he could to share scientific information with the wider world. He worked with American public television to create a television show called **COSMOS** which was all about science. Cosmos became an incredibly popular show and was watched by millions of people.

Many of today's scientists say that it was Carl and his television show that first got them interested in science. NASA thanked him for his great work by giving him the Distinguished Public Service Medal twice, in 1977 and again in 1981.

Carl died in 1996, but his work still inspires many people to look up at the stars and wonder today.

*"Somewhere, something incredible is waiting to be known."*

BORN: **c. 1864** DIED: **JANUARY 5, 1943**

# George Washington Carver was a botanist and inventor.

George was born into slavery. His parents were enslaved, which meant George was, too. At that time, the US was in the middle of a civil war over whether slavery should continue. The Civil War ended when George was still very young and slavery was made illegal. The people that had owned George and his family, Moses and Susan Carver, decided to raise George as if he was their own child.

Susan Carver started to teach George how to read and write and, when he was old enough, sent him to a school for black children in another town. The teacher at that school became a role model for George. She told him that he should learn as much as he could and then use what he learned to help other people. That lesson stayed with George his whole life.

From a very young age, George loved plants. Many people around town called him the **PLANT DOCTOR** because he would help them to take care of their plants if they were sick or not growing well.

While he was in school George spent a lot of his time studying plants. After he graduated from high school, he set up his own conservatory, a place to grow and study plants.

He worked in his conservatory while he tried to get into college. When he first applied, he was accepted because of his good grades. But, when the college found out that he was black they sent him away. George had to apply to other schools and eventually was admitted to study botany (the study of plant life) at Iowa State Agricultural College.

George was the first black student at that college in 1891. He was such a great student that when he finished his studies he became the first black teacher at the college too. This ignited his career as a researcher.

Shortly after graduating, George was invited to run the Agriculture Department at the Tuskegee Institute, a university that was built to serve black students. While he was at Tuskegee, George's research focused on finding new ways to use a wide variety of plants such as soy beans, sweet potatoes, and pecans. He also found new ways of improving soil for planting crops. He became most famous for his work on peanuts. From instant coffee to paint, mayonnaise, and shampoo, he discovered over 300 ways of using peanuts. George's inventions and recipes helped poor farmers in the South to make more money for their crops.

Usually when people invent or discover new things they get a patent to make sure that other people can't use their ideas without paying the inventor. George didn't do that. George thought that his work should benefit all people—just like his teacher taught him when he was a child.

George died in 1943 but he is remembered for his hard work to help others. Many schools in the US are now named after George in his honor.

*"Education is the key to unlock the golden door of freedom."*

George Washington Carver

# Jaime Escalante was an inspirational educator based at Garfield High School in Los Angeles.

Born in La Paz, Bolivia, both of Jaime's parents were teachers and taught him the value of education. For most of his childhood he was raised by his mother. All through school she made sure that he worked hard and learned as much as he could.

After finishing high school, Jaime briefly served in the army during the Bolivian Revolution. But he knew that he was meant to be a teacher, like his parents. As soon as he left the army, he enrolled in classes in mathematics at university.

While he was at university, he met Fabiola Tapia, a fellow student who he fell in love with and married. He also started teaching high school classes while he was still a student in college.

Jaime taught math and physics for 12 years and had two sons with his wife. But they were worried about raising sons in Bolivia because of the political and economic problems there at that time. So, in 1963, they decided to move to the US and start a new life.

When they arrived in the US, Jaime barely knew any English and didn't have very much money. But he knew he wanted to find a way to be a teacher again. He found a job mopping floors while he took classes in English and mathematics, and then worked on a degree in mathematics.

He was so good at math that he eventually got a job in electronics that paid him well. But it wasn't what he wanted to be doing. When he finally finished his education in 1974, he quit his job to take a lower-paid job as a teacher.

At his new school, many of the students were lower-income and Mexican-American students. Most of them did not know basic math. So, even though Jaime wanted to start teaching hard classes like calculus right away, he taught basic math and algebra for a few years first. He wanted to help his students get better.

Jaime made his students work hard and convinced them that they could succeed. He told them, **"I'll teach you math and that's your language. With that, you're going to make it."**

In 1978, Jaime got to teach his first calculus class to his students. He insisted that they come in after school and on Saturdays to study because he wanted them to do well. He didn't only expect *them* to work hard though. He worked very hard himself. Whenever they came in after school or on weekends that meant that he was working too. Jaime's students found his work ethic inspiring. One of them said, "If he can do it, we can do it. If he wants to teach us that bad, we can learn."

In 1982, his students did so well on a national test that many people suspected they cheated. They were asked to take the test again and still excelled because Jaime had taught them so well.

The story of Jaime's teaching was so inspiring that he was given the Medal for Excellence in Education by the President of the United States. He is remembered today as one of the best teachers that the US has ever seen.

**"YOU DO NOT ENTER THE FUTURE – YOU CREATE THE FUTURE. THE FUTURE IS CREATED THROUGH HARD WORK."**

**JAIME ESCALANTE**

CARLOS ACOSTA

BORN: **JUNE 2, 1973**

## Carlos Acosta is a ballet dancer and choreographer.

Carlos was born in Havana, Cuba. As he was growing up, his family struggled through poverty. Carlos was the youngest of 11 children and his father could not make enough money to take care of the whole family. Growing up in poverty meant that Carlos rarely had toys, sometimes didn't have shoes to wear, and often went to bed hungry.

When Carlos was about nine years old, his father decided that the best thing to do would be to send Carlos to one of the ballet schools that was run by the government. At ballet school Carlos would be fed a free lunch every day and his time in training would keep him from getting into trouble with his friends. At first Carlos really did not want to go to dance school because he was afraid his friends would make fun of him. He hated dance so much at first that he skipped a lot of his classes and got expelled! Carlos' father had no patience for this. He forced Carlos to enroll in another ballet school. This time Carlos would be on his best behavior.

Carlos kept going to ballet school and he started to get very good. By the time he graduated in 1991, he was at the top of his class and was getting attention from dance companies in North America and Europe. In 1991, he danced for the English National Ballet and then he became a member of the National Ballet of Cuba. By 1994 he was named a principal dancer in the National Ballet of Cuba, the highest rank in a dance company. He eventually settled in Houston to work as a principal dancer in the Houston Ballet for five years. Over his career, he danced all the famous roles, both classical and contemporary. He became known for his athleticism, magnetic performances, and ability to show emotion through dance.

Then, Carlos received a wonderful opportunity. He was invited to be a permanent member of **THE ROYAL BALLET** in Britain—one of the most prestigious dance companies in the world. He danced for the Royal Ballet from 1998 to 2015. During that time Carlos choreographed his own ballet, *Tocororo: A Cuban Tale*, and wrote a memoir of his life, *No Way Home: A Dancer's Journey from the Streets of Havana to the Stages of the World*. He also received a huge number of awards for his dancing, including being named a Commander of the Order of the British Empire for services to ballet.

Today Carlos continues to write books and choreograph ballet. His story inspires others going through challenges about what it is possible to achieve.

## "This art is beautiful, and someone has to do it."

# Bayard Rustin was an activist and community organizer.

Bayard was born in Westchester, Pennsylvania. He was raised by his grandparents alongside their 11 other children, growing up in a relatively large and wealthy home. Bayard's grandparents hosted a lot of guests and they had a huge impact on Bayard's life. Some of the guests that visited were leaders of movements for African-American rights such as W.E.B. Du Bois. Bayard learned about racial inequality and started working to end inequality at an early age.

When Bayard was 20 years old, he went to Wilberforce University, where he started working with other students on social issues. One of the issues he took up was the low quality of food in the cafeteria for students. He organized a student strike to try to fix the problem and was expelled for it. For Bayard this was only the beginning of what would be a long life of protest and activism.

During World War Two, Bayard organized protests about many important issues. One of those issues was the segregation of the US military—black troops were kept separate from white troops. Another issue was that the US government unfairly imprisoned 120,000 Japanese Americans during the war. Bayard worked with an organization called the *Fellowship of Reconciliation* to organize protests to address these problems.

Bayard believed strongly in refusing to use violence to solve problems. He looked to Mahatma Gandhi as an example of how to protest peacefully and engage in civil disobedience. Bayard believed so strongly in non-violence, that he refused to

register for the draft during World War Two and was eventually arrested. He was imprisoned for two years. But even while he was in prison his passion for addressing inequalities never faltered. He protested segregation in the prison.

This was not the only time that Bayard was sent to jail for doing what he believed in. In 1947 he was arrested for protesting segregated public transportation and he was forced to do hard physical labor for several weeks. He was arrested again in 1953, but this time he was arrested for being gay. Bayard was a man who loved other men and that was illegal at that time. He was imprisoned for 60 days but did not let that change who he was. Bayard refused to ever hide the fact that he was gay.

By the late 1950s Bayard had a lot of practice organizing people and coordinating protests. As Dr. Martin Luther King Jr. began to gain popularity as a civil rights leader, Bayard shared with him lessons about non-violence and civil disobedience. Bayard assisted Dr. Martin Luther King Jr. with the planning of many of the iconic protests and marches of the civil rights movement including the Montgomery Bus Boycott and the **1963 MARCH ON WASHINGTON**.

Bayard Rustin died in 1987 but he deserves a place among the most iconic activists and civil rights leaders in US history. In 2013, 26 years after Bayard's death, President Barack Obama awarded Bayard the Presidential Medal of Freedom, the highest honor the US government can give.

*"The only way to reduce ugliness in the world is to reduce it in yourself."*

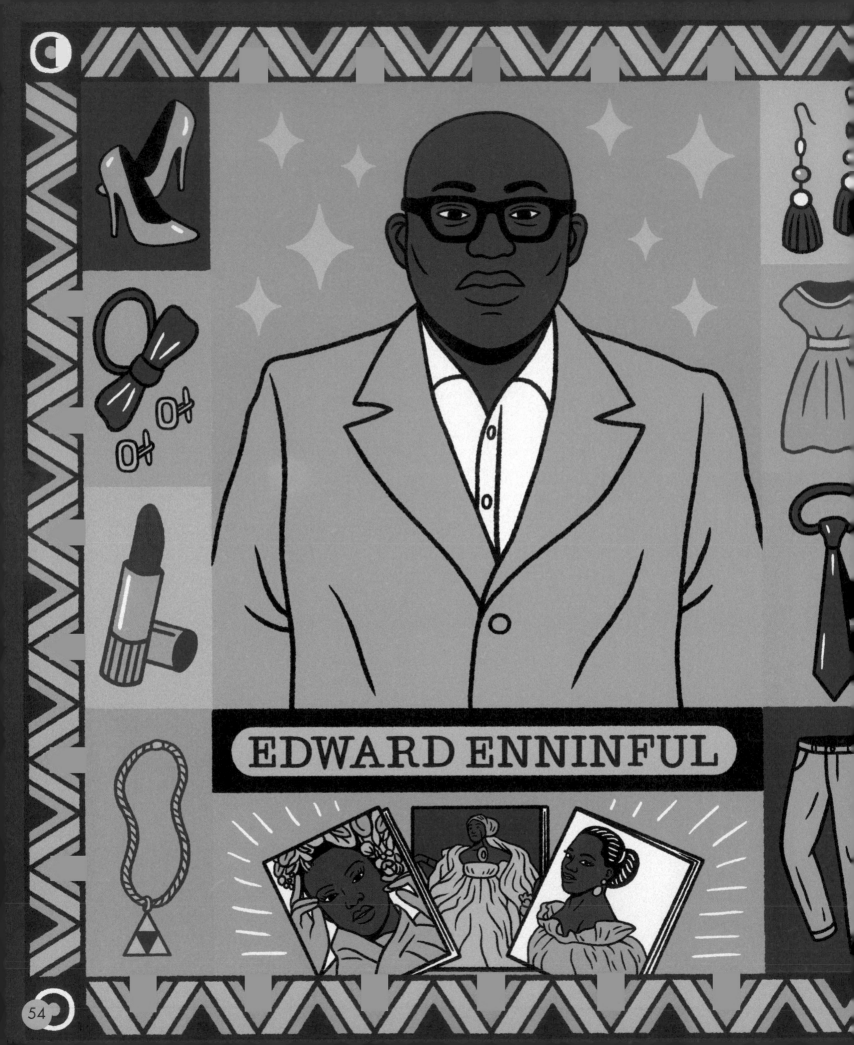

EDWARD ENNINFUL

## Edward Enninful is a fashion stylist and Editor-in-Chief of British Vogue.

Edward was born in Ghana, but when he was very young, his family moved to London. His mother was a seamstress who designed bright and beautiful clothes. This would later provide inspiration for Edward's iconic career in the fashion industry.

When Edward was at school, he never mentioned any fashion aspirations because his parents wanted him to become a lawyer. But when he was 16 years old, a man came up to him on a train in London and commented that he should be a model. That man was Simon Foxton, a stylist for a fashion magazine called *i-D*. Simon wanted to hire Edward as a model but Edward had to make sure his mom would let him first. After some convincing, she said yes.

Edward went to a few photo shoots with Simon and quickly started to get excited about fashion. He started working as Simon's assistant right away. He didn't stay as Simon's assistant for very long though. People in the fashion industry noticed how friendly Edward was and how he had great style ideas. Edward made a very good impression and in just two short years, when he was 18 years old, he became the fashion director of *i-D*. That made him the youngest fashion director ever at an international magazine.

It wasn't long before Edward started working for some of the biggest brands in the world, styling an advertising campaign for Calvin Klein when he was just 22 years old. His work at *i-D* contributed to some of the biggest trends in fashion in the 1990s, like grunge.

Edward didn't stay at *i-D* forever though. In 1998 he started working as a contributing editor for Italian Vogue, considered by many to be the top fashion magazine in the world. He also did work for *American Vogue*. In 2011 Edward became the fashion and style director for *W*, a magazine with nearly half a million readers.

In 2016, Edward's contributions to the fashion industry were recognized by the British Crown when he was named an Officer of the Most Excellent Order of the British Empire—a huge award.

And in 2017, Edward took the most prestigious job of his life so far. He became the editor-in-chief of **BRITISH VOGUE**. Edward is the first man, and person of color, to ever hold that job. His first issue was the most hotly anticipated cover in the magazine's history. Edward showed he wasn't afraid to make political statements with his coverlines and models.

Edward is considered to be one of the most influential people in fashion, He is known for his creative eye, his risk-taking mentality, and his commitment to diversity in fashion.

## "I can tell you, without diversity, creativity remains stagnant."

JOHN DEWEY

BORN: **OCTOBER 20, 1859**

DIED: **JUNE 1, 1952**

# John Dewey was a psychologist who reformed education.

When John was young he was a great student. He finished high school at an early age and then enrolled at the University of Vermont when he was only 15 years old. He graduated from college second in his class, aged 19.

John started working as a teacher. But it wasn't long before he decided he wanted to go back to school himself. He began a P.h.D. at Johns Hopkins University, which he finished in 1884.

John got a job as a professor at the University of Michigan immediately after finishing his work at Johns Hopkins. He taught at the University of Michigan for four years and in that time he met and married his first wife, Harriet Alice Chapman. John and Harriet eventually had six children and adopted a seventh.

In 1894 John moved with his family to Chicago to start a new job as the head of the philosophy department at the University of Chicago. By this time John was starting to become quite famous as a scholar for his work in the fields of philosophy, psychology, and education.

He wrote several books encouraging society to change the way it thought about education. John thought that everyone should have access to high quality education and that the best education allowed students to learn by actually *doing* things—instead of just reading about them in books.

In 1904, he moved once again – this time to New York to work at Columbia University. During that time he traveled all over the world to give lectures on his ideas about education.

Over the course of his career, John worked as President of both the American Psychological Association and the American Philosophical Association. He published about 40 books, too.

In addition to his academic work, John was also an activist. He believed that the US was becoming more economically unequal and spoke out for the rights of workers to improve their working and living conditions. He also marched for women's rights and was one of the earliest members of the NAACP.

John Dewey died in 1952, but is remembered today for trying to make the world a fairer and more equal place.

*"Education is not preparation for life; education is life itself."*

ALFRED NOBEL

# Alfred Nobel was a chemist, known for creating dynamite.

Born in Sweden, Alfred grew up in a very wealthy family. His father was an engineer and inventor who ran a business making tools and explosives. Alfred, who would eventually become a very accomplished inventor himself, followed in his father's footsteps.

In 1837, when Alfred was only about 4 years old, his father moved to Saint Petersburg to open a new business. Once the business started to do well, in 1842, the rest of Alfred's family moved there to join him. Because business was booming, Alfred's family could afford to hire private tutors. Working with tutors helped Alfred tremendously. He managed to learn four different languages and became excellent at chemistry.

He became so good at chemistry, in fact, that he was able to spend some of his youth studying with the most prominent chemists in Europe at the time. One of the chemists that he got to work with was Ascanio Sobrero. Ascanio had just invented nitroglycerine. Nitroglycerine is dangerous because it explodes very easily in response to heat or pressure. Ascanio thought it was a bad idea to work with nitroglycerine, but Alfred was determined to find a way to make it safe to work with.

The desire to make nitroglycerine safe inspired Alfred to work harder than ever before. He filed his first patent (a certification of a new invention) in 1857 and more quickly followed. He filed patents for many tools related to explosives, including a detonator and a blasting cap.

In 1867, Alfred finally achieved what he set out to do. He invented **DYNAMITE**, an explosive that was safer than nitroglycerine but just as effective. Dynamite became an incredibly important tool for mining, demolition, and many other things, but dynamite was also useful for making weapons.

Over the next two decades Alfred became extremely wealthy as his business did very well. But in 1888, one of Alfred's brothers—Ludvig—passed away. When Ludvig died some newspapers made a mistake and thought that Alfred had died. They ran stories about Alfred and some of them called him the "merchant of death" because his businesses made so many weapons. Alfred was not happy that people thought of him that way and was determined to make people remember him differently.

In order to do this, he decided that when he died most of his money would go to set up the **NOBEL PRIZES.** The Nobel Prizes are awards given every year to people anywhere in the world who make substantial contributions to science, literature, and international peace.

Alfred's efforts worked. Today Alfred is remembered as a great scientist who was inducted into the Royal Swedish Academy of Sciences and who had 355 patented inventions by the time he died in 1896. And, his last name, Nobel, is a symbol of human achievement in the sciences, arts, and in efforts for peace.

*"Good wishes alone will not ensure peace."*

ALFR. NOBEL

NAT. MDCCC XXXIII OB. MDCCC XCVI

## Kit Yan is a poet and playwright

Kit was born in Enping, China, but moved to t[he]
Kingdom of Hawaii as a baby. Kit's interest in t[he]
power of words started at a very young age. Kit wro[te]
poems in elementary school about how complicat[ed]
friendships were on the playground and how growing [up]
often came with a lot of complex feelings. The first time [Kit]
remembers performing poetry in front of an audience w[as]
with some friends when they were around eight years o[ld.]
Together they memorized the lines of a poem by Shel Silverste[in]
called *Peanut-Butter Sandwich*. They even added choreography[.]

According to Kit, their love of telling stories and using words to s[tir]
up emotions in others came from growing up in a culture where stori[es]
and emotions were very important. Kit learned, especially from stro[ng]
women in the community, to use stories and the power of the spoken wo[rd]
to have an impact on others. Kit also started to be critical of the expectatio[ns]
we have of girls and boys from an early age. In elementary and high scho[ol]
Kit sung in choirs. Kit noticed that boys and girls were assigned different pa[rts]
to sing based on their gender instead of on how their voices actually sounde[d.]
At that point Kit was considered by many to be a girl and was expected to si[ng]
the girl's parts, but that didn't match Kit's identity.

Kit didn't like the rules about gender and eventually quit
the choir because the parts didn't match how Kit
wanted to perform.

When Kit was
8 years old they moved
to Massachusetts (a long way from home!) to
attend college. The original plan for a college
education was for Kit to study business and become
an entrepreneur. But, in Kit's first year of college
they attended a poetry slam, a competition between
poets where they perform poetry out loud in front of an
audience. That event was very inspiring for Kit who then
decided to join a poetry team and work to develop their
writing and performance skills.

Kit didn't stop studying business though. After graduating with
a degree in business, Kit combined business knowledge with a
passion for poetry and performance, to begin building a career
as a poet. They started traveling all over to perform poetry for
audiences that would benefit from hearing the stories Kit had to share.
Kit uses poetry to inspire emotions about gender, race, and inequalities
in society. Many of Kit's poems are stories of their own experience of
questioning and challenging rules about gender and coming out as a
transgender man.

*"If you want to wear Mom's clothes to school or a suit or a*
*costume... they're all just costumes so use them to make yourself*
*feel beautiful."*

W.E.B. DU BOIS

## W.E.B. Du Bois was an activist, author, and historian.

William Edward Burghardt Du Bois, also known as W.E.B. Du Bois, was born in Massachusetts. His family was one of the very few free black families in his town at that time. His father left when he was very young and his mother worked hard to support the family.

At that time many of the schools in the US were segregated by law, so many black children had to go to schools that were not as good as the schools white children could go to. Those laws were not in place in Massachusetts, so W.E.B. was able to go to the same local school as white children.

W.E.B. did very well in elementary and high school, but he could not afford to go to college. However, the people at his local church knew that he was a very promising student and raised money to pay for him to go. So, in 1885, W.E.B. started attending Fisk University in Nashville, Tennessee.

While he was in Tennessee, W.E.B. saw racial inequality like he had never seen before. Tennessee at that time still had many laws that required black and white people to be separated. Laws were also put in place to try to prevent black people from voting and there was a lot of racist violence. W.E.B. saw this inequality and recognized that things needed to change. This experience inspired him to spend a lifetime studying and working to address racism.

In 1888, W.E.B. left Tennessee and moved back to Massachusetts to study at Harvard University, where he received a bachelor's degree in history. He went on to enroll in the sociology Ph.D. program at Harvard and became the first African American to receive a doctorate from Harvard in 1895.

After graduating W.E.B. started working as a professor and as an outspoken advocate for equal rights for black people in America. In 1909 he became one of the founders of the NAACP. He also wrote books and gave public speeches insisting that black people should have full rights in the US. He protested unjust laws and discrimination.

In addition to his work as an activist, W.E.B. became a leading academic. He did revolutionary academic work on inequality in new and exciting ways. Some of his books, such as **SOULS OF BLACK FOLK** are still considered to be some of the most important books written in US history.

Unfortunately, W.E.B. did not live to see the effect of his work. He died a year before the Civil Rights Act was passed, which made many of the changes he had been fighting for.

*"The power of the ballot we need in sheer defense, else what shall save us from a second slavery?"*

Dedicated to Stewart Leek. To some he was a teacher, a poet, a friend, a brother, a husband, or a father. To me he was a grandfather and the best role model a grandson could ever ask for. —C.L.

Dedicated to my girlfriend, Ronja, who always has my back in stressful times and to our son, Jasper, who was born while I was working on this book. I love you and I owe you both so much! —B.R.

Brimming with creative inspiration, how-to projects, and useful information to enrich your everyday life, Quarto Knows is a favourite destination for those pursuing their interests and passions. Visit our site and dig deeper with our books into your area of interest: Quarto Creates, Quarto Cooks, Quarto Homes, Quarto Lives, Quarto Drives, Quarto Explores, Quarto Gifts, or Quarto Kids.

Boy Oh Boy © 2019 Quarto Publishing plc. Text © 2019 Clifford Leek. Illustrations © 2019 Bene Rohlmann.

First Published in 2019 by Wide Eyed Editions, an imprint of The Quarto Group. 400 First Avenue North, Suite 400, Minneapolis, MN 55401, USA. T (612) 344-8100 F (612) 344-8692 **www.QuartoKnows.com**

The right of Bene Rohlmann to be identified as the illustrator and Clifford Leek to be identified as the author of this work has been asserted by them in accordance with the Copyright, Designs and Patents Act, 1988 (United Kingdom).

ISBN 978-1-78603-875-3

The illustrations were created digitally
Set in Futura, Lobster Two, and Intro Bold

Published by Rachel Williams and Jenny Broom
Designed by Karissa Santos
Edited by Katy Flint
Production by Nicolas Zeifman

Manufactured in China
9 8 7 6 5 4 3 2 1